My Favorite Teammate Is The Kid Named Jesus

My Favorite Teammate Is The Kid Named Jesus

Brett Payne

Copyright © 2019 by Brett Payne

ISBN 9781970160161 Ebook
ISBN 9781970160208 Paperback

All rights reserved. No part of this publication may be reproduced, distributed, or transmitted in any form or by any means, including photocopying, recording, or other electronic or mechanical methods without the prior written permission of the publisher. For permission requests, solicit the publisher via the address below through mail or email with the subject line "Attention: Publication Permission".

EC Publishing LLC
11100 SW 93rd Court Road, Suite 10-215
Ocala, Florida 34481-5188, USA

www.ecpublishingllc.com
info@ecpublishingllc.com
+1 (352) 234-6201

Printed in the United States of America

CHAPTER 1

Our basketball team, the Kingston Lionhearts, was struggling to stay in contention for the playoffs. We were three quarters of the way through the season and had just lost six straight games.

At our next practice, Coach H.S. Love gathered the players together and said, "I've got good news for you guys."

Then he waved at a kid to come over, who was practicing shots across the court.

He said, "Guys, I want to introduce you to Jesus, your new teammate. I believe that he's got just what we need to overcome at such a time as this."

So that's when we first met Jesus. And Coach Love wasn't kidding about his abilities. He was a good passer, a real good communicator, and a great team player. From that point on, our team had new life!

Now, let me tell you a little bit about our team. My name is Johnny Lightning.

Some of the kids joke around about my name because lightning is usually associated with being fast. But I am really kind of slow. I'm a bit pudgy and I have short legs. It's all good though, they're just having fun.

Except, when some of the meaner kids in the neighborhood see me, they say, "Here comes oxymoron".

At first I thought they were calling me a moron, until I asked my mother what it meant. She explained that an oxymoron is when you have two words together, that actually have opposite meanings. Words such as, "bittersweet", or "jumbo shrimp", or "skinny broad". Then I understood their reasoning. To them, Johnny meant slowpoke and lightning meant speedy. The two really don't go together. Oh well, even though it hurts a little, it is kind of funny.

The position I play is usually the bench. But I do have a fairly good three point shot if I'm not being covered well. So coach Love often puts me in if we need a lot of points in a hurry. Since I don't look like much of a basketball player, I can get quite a few shots off before the other team realizes that this guy is not a bad shooter.

Then there's my brother Jimmy. He's twelve, a year older than me. He plays forward. Jimmy's a much better athlete than I am and he's certainly not as chubby.

Pauley Possel is the other forward. Pauley's not afraid of anything. He uses his frame very well in driving to the net, and on defense, he holds his ground and doesn't flinch when someone is driving toward him.

He's constantly taking a beating while sacrificing his body in order to get a charging call. And also, when he's trying to get us the ball back by diving for it. One of our guards is Barney Grace, a very consistent and talented player, and a great defender. He is always very generous with the ball, often passing to other players when he has an open shot of his own.

Then, of course, there's our center and team leader, Pete Bolder. Pete's our tallest player at almost six feet, and he's solid too, strong as an ox. Pete's method of playing is to give one hundred and ten percent effort on every play, all the time. He's like a machine, he never seems to get tired. He also pushes the rest of us to play with all our hearts, to never give up. Pete is the most bold and courageous player

I've ever met. And to round off the starting team, is Jesus at point guard.

Now, after Jesus joined our team, we didn't lose any more games. In fact, we won all seven of the rest of our regular season games, made the playoffs, and then won the quarter and semifinal games. Even though both of those games were really close and could have gone either way, the team pulled together and fought for victory.

Our team, the Lionhearts, was now going to play in the League Championship Snow game, our first one ever. Our opponents were the Salem Saints. They had already won the previous two championships.

For the first time this season, many of our players appeared to be very nervous.

The Saints did have three players that were even taller than Pete.

After the warm-ups, we were all in the locker room, when Jesus stood up and said, "No matter how this game turns out, I want all of you to know that I am very grateful to be a member of this team. I am sincerely thankful of the friendships I have with every one of you. Now I believe that we can win this game if we just stay focused on what we do best, and that is, to play as a team, to do what's best for the team." Coach Love then gathered us close together. As we all took a knee he said, "Boys, you made an incredible comeback this season. All of the teams in the league are very impressed. But in order to be totally triumphant, we need just one more win." "Now, listen up. Here's our strategy. Everyone get the ball to Pete as often as possible.

The Saints have some tall players but they're not nearly as strong as Pete. He'll muscle the ball right through them. Now let's go give it all you've got! Leave nothing on the court! Go, boys, go!"

And that's just what we did. Everyone scored points in the first half. But Pete scored twice as many as all of the rest of us. He was awesome! Every time he touched the ball he scored. At half time we were up by five points.

We went into the second half feeling loose and confident. Things started out well, But then it happened.

Pete was forcing the ball to the net and was fouled hard by the Saint's biggest man. Though he still made the basket, when he came down, he landed on another defender and twisted his ankle. Pete was in so much pain Coach Love took him out of the game.

Without our best scorer, the Saints came back quickly. Before we knew it, they were up by nine points. Even though Pete was badly hurting, he was pacing the sidelines, begging Coach Love to put him back in the game.

Then coach called a timeout. We only had about a minute left in the game.

Coach Love said, "I'm putting you back in Pete but don't worry about scoring so much. Just play defense and try to get some rebounds. I don't want you injured any worse.

Then he said, "Johnny, you're going in too. Just concentrate and do your thing, son." It didn't take long after we brought the ball in for me to get a pass from Jesus and an open shot. Whooosh! A thirty footer!

The Saints came back and drove for what looked like an easy lay-up, but Pete, appeared out of nowhere and stuffed it! A blocked shot!

Jesus passed me the ball again, this time on the left side. I focused and let it fly.

Swish! Another three pointer!

The Saints brought it back down and drove again to their net. This time Pauley was there, his feet set firm. He drew the charging penalty!

Even though a giant Saint ran right over him, landing on Pauley, crushing him to the floorboards, Pauley just rolled over, stood up, brushed himself off, and trotted to the foul line. He sunk both shots!

Now, there was only five seconds left and the Saints were up by one point. They call a timeout. Coach Love made his instructions very simple for us. He said, "Just steal the ball and shoot!"

Because there was so little time left, I expected the Saints to make their inbound pass far down the court in order to waste a few seconds. And that's just what happened. While discreetly waiting at half court, I was able to beat their man to the pass. Immediately, I saw Jesus open in the lane, about ten feet from the basket. I hurled it to him.

Jesus drove to the net. There were three big Saints right under it. Jesus went left as if to try a lay-up on that side. Then, just as all the Saints jumped to block it, he rolled the ball to his right hand and flipped it to Pete, who had already jumped as high as he ever had before!

Pete slammed a dunk right into the basket! The ball ricocheted back and forth inside the rim at least ten times! Bam! Bam! Bam! Bam! Bam! Bam! Bam! Bam!
Bam! Bam!
Then, horribly, the ball flew right out of the top of the net! The buzzer sounds!
The Saints win by one point.

I felt as though someone had just punched me right in the gut. We had worked so hard and were so close to winning it. Everyone on the team was stunned. That is, except for Jesus. While we were all sulking and moaning, just standing around with our heads down, Jesus was happily congratulating the Saint players, shaking hands, high fiving them, patting some on the back and hugging others.

As we were walking back to the locker room, my brother Jimmy asked Jesus, "Why are you so joyful? Do you know those other players? Why are you treating them so nice?"

Jesus said, "Whatever does it matter whether I know them or not, Jimmy? They played a great game. They deserved to win. Therefore, they should be honored. I believe that you should always treat people just like you would want to be treated."

"Have you ever heard anyone say, "What goes around comes around,' or 'You reap what you sow? If you do good, good things will happen to you. It works the same way if you do bad. I choose to do good."

"My father taught me that doing good is like planting a seed. Say you plant a cherry seed. Eventually, after some time, a big cherry tree grows and you get a great big harvest. I would much rather get a great big good harvest than a great big bad harvest. So, I believe that when we have the opportunity, it is a wise thing to do good, every chance we get."

When we got back to the locker room, Pete was bent over, sitting on the floor, far from the rest of the team. Jesus approached him and said, "What's the matter Pete? You played an outstanding game." Pete groaned, "You gave me a chance and I blew it. I let you down. I let the whole team down. Jesus, you should be the captain and leader of this team, not me."

Jesus responded, "Pete, cheer up man! You are a pillar and the backbone of this team! You have a sure and steadfast foundation! You are as strong and solid as a rock! In fact, I'm giving you a nickname. Do you mind if we call you 'Rocky' from now on?"

Pete then straightened up and said, "Thanks Jesus, you're pretty cool. But, you know, you're about the most gracious kid I've ever met."

Coach Love gathered us close together and congratulated each one of us with a good word and said that we have no reason to be ashamed. He said that we played a great game and that we would have many future opportunities to win championships.

He then encouraged us all to, "Be strong and courageous and hold your heads up high because you are a mighty valiant team of genuine winners!"

CHAPTER 2

It seemed like a really long wait after basketball season but finally it was springtime and baseball season had arrived. Coach Love was happy to see that all the Lionhearts were sticking together and he said that we have a great chance of going all the way. Rocky Bolder's ankle had healed and that's a good thing because he's our best pitcher. He's so big and strong that just his hulk of a presence on the pitchers causes many batters to fear. He pitches a smokin' fastball and he has a good changeup too, which tricks a lot of batters into swinging early.

My brother Jimmy plays first base, Barney plays second, and Pauley plays third.

Just like in basketball, Pauley gives up his body to stop hard hit balls in case they take a bad bounce. Not many get by him. Because he can cover a lot of ground, Jesus is our center fielder. He has soft hands which catch everything that comes his way. And he has mighty cannon of a right arm. He throws out everyone who tries to test him by taking an extra base.

Me, Johnny, I play catcher. Since I'm already short, I don't have to squat down very far to give the pitcher a target. I really like wearing the catcher's mask too. It sort of makes me look like a knight. Well, we started off the season real well. We won almost every game until about half way through when we began to choke a bit. We had lost six games in a row.

That's when Coach Love said that we looked sloppy and confused and everyone seemed to be doing his own thing. That we were making way to many mistakes and bad decisions. He said that for the good of the team, we were going back to the basics that we were going to re-learn all the fundamentals. Coach Love then spent special time with each one of us, individually, to retrain us in batting skills, fielding and throwing skills, and base running skills.

Of course, Coach Love is an extraordinary teacher, he's always optimistic, and he's never wrong. His decision to go back to the fundamentals truly did work. He needed to remind us again of everything we had learned in the past. We won our last seven games and finished first in our region. We were now going to play in the County Championship!

Since we had the better record, we were hosting the Rome Raiders at our home field. On the Raiders team there were quite a few players that were real fast. That was of concern to me because I figured that they would be trying to steal a lot of bases and it was my responsibility as catcher to throw them out. Coach love encouraged me by saying that I have a strong right arm and he advised me to just concentrate on the base and to get the ball there as quickly as possible when they try to steal. I told him I'd do my best.

Well, both teams started out playing pretty well and the score was tied two to two after two. Jesus led off the third inning and slammed the first pitch to the right field corner, all the way to the fence. He rounded first base, then second. He was going for a triple and surely would have made it in time. But the Raider shortstop, very subtly, stuck out his foot as Jesus passed by and tripped him. Jesus fell down hard, face first in the dirt, stirring up a big cloud of dust!
We all yelled, "He tripped him!"

But it was to no avail because the umpire never saw it. He was watching the ball as it was being thrown to third base. The Raiders third baseman then ran over to Jesus as he lay there and tagged him out. Jesus just got up and trotted back to the dugout. Jimmy said, "Wow, Jesus. Are you just going to let that guy get away with tripping you?"

Jesus responded, "Jimmy, do you have any idea what that guy's going through in life? Maybe he's having family problems. Or possibly he's doing poorly in school and has a lot of pressure on him. Or it could be that he's not getting along with his teammates.

It's not my will to condemn him."

"My dad says that if you judge others, you are liable to be judged yourself. Since that's the case, I think it's much smarter to show mercy."

Then he asked, "Jimmy, have you ever made a mistake?"

Jimmy was silent.

Jesus said, "I thought so. That's ok Jimmy, I'm not going to judge you either."

The raiders scored three more runs in next few innings, to our two, and were now ahead five to four, with two outs in the sixth. A Raider batter had just hit a double and was taking a big lead off of second base.

That's when Coach Love signaled for a pitchout. A pitchout is when the pitcher throws the ball really quick to the catcher, away from the batter, in order for the catcher to have a better chance to throw out the runner, when he is trying to steal.

From the dugout, Coach Love said, "Hey Johnny." He then touched his hat, folded his arms, and spit. That was our signal for a pitchout. So before I squatted down, I signaled to Rocky. I touched my hat, folded my arms, and then spit.

Instantly, I gasped the words, "Oh, Oh!"

The batter that was up was a big stocky guy with bulging biceps and forearms that looked like crab claws. He had a giant, supersized head and whole bunch more hair on his face then most kids our age.

The number on his uniform was number one. I imagined that his teammates would let him have any number he wanted. Well, I had just spit on the guy's shoe!

He took one look at his foot, frowned, then glared in anger. Suddenly he took a step toward me and reared back his bat as if he was going to knock my block off! The umpire bravely stepped in between us.
I hollered, "Sorry man! It was an accident!"
He muttered something that I'm not allowed to repeat.
Well, that was more than a little bit scary. But Rocky got the signal. He threw an outside fastball, right as the runner took off for third. I focused and zipped the ball right to the corner of the bag, catching the runner by a full two feet! Out number three! Inning Over.
I don't know how he does it but Coach Love seems to know the future before it happens and he's always willing to reveal it to us. If we could only catch all of his signals.
Our team, the Lionhearts, was unable to score in the bottom of the sixth and wewere now in the last inning of the game. Big Raider number one was leading off and he hit a line drive double off the center field fence. Jesus made a fantastic throw to third to keep the runner back.

The next player grounded out to Barney, who made a great play to get the out, but the runner advanced. With the next batter up, I could see out at the corner of my eye, big Raider number one taking a long lead off of third base. He was snorting and growling and pounding his fist into his hand. He, no doubt, really wanted a piece of me. On the first pitch from Rocky the batter squared up to bunt the ball. I immediately thought, "Oh, no! It's s suicide squeeze play!"
A suicide squeeze is when the runner on third base takes off running toward home plate as the ball is pitched. The batter is expected to hit the ball or to lay down a bunt, no matter what. The catcher, on defense, is expected to block home plate with his body and to wait

for a throw, even though the runner has a great jump and is already barreling toward him at full speed.

The batter made a perfect bunt. The ball rolled left, between Rocky and the third base line. I planted myself in front of home plate as what looked like a steam train was charging fast, right at me. Rocky dove for the ball with his bare right hand and in one motion flipped it at me.

Just as I caught the ball I was unmercifully drilled and everything went black for an instant. I rolled three backwards somersaults and ended up sprawled put on my butt, flat against the backstop. I was feeling quite dazed as the umpire lifted up my glove.
Miraculously, the ball was still in it!
He yelled, "Ooooout!"

All my teammates shouted like madmen! Big number one limped off the field, cursing under his breath. I was able to get up and pull it together and Rocky struck out the last batter.
It was now the bottom of the last inning and we were still down by one run.
Jimmy leads off and he hits a long fly ball all the way to the warning track. But the Raider center fielder makes a remarkable catch. One out, I'm up next.
Since I'm pretty short, my strike zone is small, so I get a lot of walks. When I do get a good pitch, I can usually hit it somewhere.
The first pitch was a ball. The second another ball. The third as well. I'm now three and looking for a walk. The next pitch was high, right at my eye level, I threw down my bat and headed to first.

Then I hear the umpire, "Striiiike!"
I'm thinking, "Oh, come on ump, you've got to be kidding." But I kept my mouth shut.
The following pitch was in the dirt.
"Striiiike!"

I'm like, "OK, that's how it's going to be." Alright, now I'm three and two and must guard the plate, or else. The next pitch was high, but not wanting to take a chance on another called strike, I smacked at it. The ball bloops right over the third basemen's head. A base hit!

Barney's up next. He hits one bouncer line drive to center field. Now there's a man on first and second, one out. Next batter's Pauley. He lines up close to the plate. He gets an inside pitch. It hits him square in the back! Pauley takes another lump for the team. Now the bases are loaded.

Next up is Jesus. He looks over toward me at third and gives me a thumbs up.

On the first pitch he slams a fly ball high and hard to center field. It looks like it could be a home run. Even if it's caught, all I have to do is to tag up on third and make it home to tie the score.

With his back to the fence, the Raider center field jumps as high as he can. He reaches up. He stretches out. Sensationally, he comes down with the ball!

I've got one foot on third base as I hear everyone yell, "Go Johnny Go!"

I take off to home plate as fast as I can. The center fielder makes a spectacular relay throw to the Raider shortstop. But I'm almost home.

Then, ten feet from home plate, without warning, I stumble! My body is moving forward but my feet can't keep up! I hit the ground, frantically crawling on all fours!

Dirt's flying everywhere!

Right as I dive for the score, the throw hits the catcher's mitt! He tags me out with just inches to go! Astounding double play! Lionhearts lose, Raiders win.

As the Raiders began to celebrate, I just lay there, prone on my face, feeling sick, defeated, a failure.

Somebody grabs me, picks me up, and shakes me! It's Jesus!

He says, "I've never seen such vigorous driven hustle, such fervent unyielding determination, in all my life! What a champion!"

He hugs me. He says, "Johnny, I love you man! You're the best! You are special!

He then went over to congratulate the Raider center fielder for playing a great game.

As I stood there, I heard a strange sound coming from our bench. I looked over and was amazed to see that all of my teammates and Coach Love were standing in a row in front of our dugout. They were all clapping their hands in unison.

When the Raiders saw what was happening, they stopped celebrating and lined up in front of their dugout. They began to clap along with us in unison.

Then Rocky Bolder shouted, "Long live the Raiders!"

The whole Raider team returned with, "Long live the Lionhearts!"

Both teams then ran onto the field with respect and appreciation for one another, jumping up and down, laughing and celebrating, together!

As our squad gathered after all the fun, every one of my teammates gave me a high five, a handshake, and a hug along with comforting words like, "You're a competitor, Johnny; we really appreciate you; you are the man!"

Last of all, Coach Love put his hands on my shoulders, looked me straight in the eyes, and said, "Johnny, I wouldn't trade you for anyone in the world. You are a member of this team of victors, of this close-nit family of high achieving champions forever. Son, you truly have a lion's heart!"

CHAPTER 3

It turned out to be a really hot summer, but I didn't care. That's cause Jimmy and me went on vacation at the beach for a whole month! Our Grandma has a house there and she invites us and our cousins to come every summer. We go swimming every day. We also go fishing, and crabbing, and clam digging, and sailing. We just have a blast of a good time. You can't beat it!

But soon it was August and football season. We were truly happy to be back to work for the team effort. Coach H.S. Love seemed to be extra excited this year. He said that with hard work, perseverance, and teamwork, we would be sure to go far!

Naturally, Rocky is our quarterback. Not only does he have a great throwing arm, but he's a tough runner too. With his size and power, he sometimes runs over defensive linemen as though they're not even there. He's also our middle linebacker.

Jesus plays wide receiver. He is supernaturally fast and can really jump high to catch the ball in a crowd. And he always brings it down. He can indeed take a hit and nothing gets away from him. He never fumbles. He never lets go. Jesus also plays free safety on defense.

Pauley's our fullback. Occasionally he runs the ball but mostly he leads the way blocking for Barney. As is his nature, Pauley sacrifices his body like a battering ram, busting through tacklers, creating a path for Barney to run through. Anybody can tell that he takes a beating because he always has the most marks on his helmet.

Barney, at tailback, is constantly twisting and turning, wrestling and pounding forward, in order to get every possible inch he can out of every run. Barney is always physical, focused, and confident. He'd rather take on all eleven defenders than to run out of bounds. He's also quick to give Pauley the credit for blocking so well when he scores.

He and Pauley work very well together.

My brother Jimmy plays tight end. He's a very good blocker and he has good hands. He's pretty fearless, too.

Myself, I play guard on the line. Since my fingers are sort of short and stubby.

I'm not a very good ball handler. And as I revealed earlier, I'm no rocketboy when it comes to speed. So the line is the right position for me.

Coach Love says that even though I am not very fast, I do move very quickly out of my stance and usually hit the opposing player before he hits me. He explained that the design of our offense is perfect for small, quick guards like me. That's because we run a lot of trap plays in which all the linemen block down a man on the defense, allowing one man to freely come through untouched, right where the running back is headed. The guard on the other side pulls, which means that he runs straight down the line where the other blockers just left, then rudely surprises the defender, who thought that he had a free shot at tackling the runner.

I get a whole bunch of good, hard hits that way and knock down many kids that are more than twice my size. Now that really makes me feel like a warrior!

We also run a good deal of sweeps where the guard pulls and leads the runner around the end. Because I'm so short and round, I can easily bowl down the defenders just as if they're bowling pins. Football is definitely my favorite sport!

MY FAVORITE TEAMMATE IS THE KID NAMED JESUS

After a full month of long, hard practices in the steamy August weather, our season finally began. Our team, the Kingston Lionhearts, played our first game against a team of very large corn-fed farm boys called the Dairyland Creamers. Well, we creamed them.

Next we played the Hampton Smokers. We smoked them.

Our third game was against the Orangeburg Crushers. What do you think we did?

We crushed them.

We just kept winning! All the sweat and toil we suffered in August was paying off. Every player was assigned their own special job to do and every man was fulfilling their work for the common good of the whole team.

Coach love was very enthusiastic. He called our Lionheart team, "A relentless, dominating force of extreme power!"

Our hope, our faith, our strength, our confidence level just kept growing with every victory. Before we knew it, we had completed the whole season undefeated, and had won the honor of playing in the State Championship Game at the State Capital!

We were all really excited to play in the big game but Coach Love warned us that the opposing team was also undefeated. He said that team had a history of doing whatever it takes to win, rules or no rules. The team was feared due to their deceptive practices and violent tactics. The players were well trained to be brutally vicious, blatantly malicious, and obscenely cruel.

The team we were about to contest were the dreaded Southside Blue Demons, and their coach, the haughty, dubious, disdainful, depraved, Lou Sypher!

On the night of the big game the stadium was packed. The Lionhearts ran onto the field to a great, roaring cheer of the crowd. Then the Blue Demons were announced.

As the Blue Demons ran onto the field a great, dark cloud covered the stadium. Then blew a mighty, whipping gust of wind and a deafening crack of thunder. The stadium lights flickered off an on.

When the wind ceased the whole place was quiet, dark, and gloomy. Only about a third of the lights remained on. An announcement was made that a powerful tornado had just swept through downtown main street.

It seemed to me to be a bit more than coincidental that the storm hit just as the Blue demons took the field. You would expect that the fans would go home to check their property, but no one left. Apparently shocked and stunned, they all stayed in their seats. The officials decided to begin the game.

The Blue Demon players were unbelievably enormous. They also looked fiercely intimidating in their all black uniforms. The Lionhearts realized that we had more than a game on our hands. This would be no playtime. This would be a fight. This would be a battle!

We kicked off first and the Demons got a good return. It didn't take them long to drive down the field for the first score. Now it was our turn.

In the huddle, Jesus reminded us to just focus on our assignments and to give it our all.

We moved the ball slowly, but surely and consistently, up the field. On first down we'd usually run a trap play up the middle. On second, we'd run an off tackle or a sweep.

On third down Rocky would hit Jesus on a slant pass over the middle. We were pounding it right down their throats, little by little.

Then directly, right into the endzone! Jesus scored on a quick slant to tie the game. This is the way the game proceeded throughout the first half. Even though Jesus was being triple covered, he caught every pass Rocky threw him. After a while, it became obvious that the Blue Demons were trying to injure Jesus, to knock him out of the game.

Certainly their wicked, conniving, morbidly deranged coach put them up to it.

Since every catch Jesus made was essential for us to keep the ball moving, the Blue Demons were gang tackling him, sometimes ruthlessly piling on six, seven, eight players, even after he was down.

They were throwing their elbows and ramming their knees into Jesus' head, his back, his ribs, his legs. They were slapping, and poking, and punching, and pounding him.

The referees must have been blind because they didn't call a single penalty. They may as well have stayed home. After a bruising first half the score was 21-21. Jesus had scored all three touchdowns for us.

As we departed the field the Demons coach ran out and stuck crooked his finger into Coach Love's chest and blurted, "Hey stud. Your chief boy is history!"

That sounded really mean, but I had no idea what it meant.

When we grouped together at halftime Jesus encouraged us, "You men are playing real tough defense. Rocky, you're right on with the passes. Way to run that ball, Barney. Great blocking linemen. Keep it up guys!"

Then Rocky asked, "Jesus, why do you always say and do things that make all the rest of us to look good? You're always praising others. Don't you like to take some credit for yourself?"

Jesus answered, "My father taught me to do this. He says to always honor and highly esteem others as though they are better, more important, and more valuable than yourself. He says that there is no greater love than this, that a man lay down his life for his friends. All you guys are my friends."

Then Jimmy said, "Hey Jesus. You're always talking about your father. Why doesn't he ever come to the games?" Jesus replied, "My father always comes to our games. He also teaches me, and coaches me, and encourages me, and he tells me exactly what I should do." Jimmy asked, "Well, why don't we ever see him?"

Jesus explained, "Well, you see, my Daddy lives in heaven. But he also lives in my heart. He's always with me. He's the best father I could ever want."

The Lionhearts began the second half with the taste of victory in our mouths. But the Blue Demon defense had really tightened up and we soon had trouble moving the ball. Our own defense was holding them as well. That is, until with about five minutes to go in the fourth quarter. The Demons called a trick play.

With third down on their own forty yard line, the Demon coach sent in six substitute players. Six ran off the field.

What we didn't notice was that one of the substitutes did not report to the huddle.

Instead, he stepped just over the out of bounds line, onto the field. As the ball was snapped, he ran down the line towards the endzone. Their quarterback threw a quick pass right to him. He was wide open. No one had covered him. We never saw him.

The Blue Demons scored an easy touchdown and with the extra point, were now up by seven. Our guys were really angry for letting the Demons get away with that. We received the kickoff and marched the ball quickly up the field. We made most of our yardage by Rocky connecting with Jesus on short passes.

As in the first half, the Demon players were ganging up on Jesus and piling on after the whistle was blown.

You could hear their coach, Lou Sypher, loudly barking from the sideline, "Hit him again, hit him again, hit him again, again, again, again!"

The pain and fatigue must have finally been getting to Jesus because he appeared to be getting up more slowly after each catch and tackle.

With third down and goal on the Demon ten yard line, Rocky once again calls on Jesus. Another slant over the middle.

The play starts well, good blocking, a great pass. Just as Jesus steps across the goal, reaching out for the reception, three Blue Demons ram their helmets right into his, knocking him flat on his back!

We all yell, "Pass interference!"

But there was no call, no flag. The referees were not only blind, but deaf too. We had to settle for a field goal.

On the next kickoff, the Demons got a good return, all the way to the fifty yard line. I don't think anyone expected them to pass on first down, except for Jesus. He blitzed from his safety position into their backfield and sacked the quarterback for a ten-yard loss.

Jesus then extended his hand to help the guy up, but the Demon grabbed a handful of dirt and threw it right in his face. Some of their linemen spit on him. Jesus just smiled and calmly walked back to the huddle.

On the next play the Demons try to play it safe. They throw a quick down and out pass toward the sideline. But Jesus is on to them. He quickly steps in front of their receiver. He intercepts the pass. The Demon receiver grabs Jesus' facemask. He rips his helmet right off! Jesus bolts toward the goal without it!

He's savagely pounded at the forty, but keeps going. Rudely smacked again at the thirty-five. He bounces off. On the thirty he's whipped around the neck. He gets loose. At the twenty-five, a gruesome shot to his face. He presses forward. Then at the twenty, the rest of the Demon team brutally hammers him with their helmets, one blow after another, even though his helmet has come off!

Jesus struggled to get up. I retrieved his helmet. I brought it to him in the huddle.

His face had been pummeled. His nose was bleeding. He had huge, nasty gashes on his forehead, his cheeks, his chin.

Jesus immediately snaps his helmet back on and proclaims, "Let's finish this!"

Now we're on the nineteen yard line with a minute to go. We run a trap up the middle for a few yards. Then an off tackle that got a couple. With little time left and only one timeout, we try a sweep. But it doesn't go far.

Once again we're on the Demon ten yard line, but now, with only five seconds to go in the game, and we need a touchdown to win. We call the timeout.

In the huddle all eyes are focused on Jesus. His face was absolutely covered in blood. His hands and sleeves were bloody from wiping his face. The blood was dripping onto his pants and his shoes. He was one big bloody mess. You couldn't even tell it was him. Jesus appeared to know exactly what all of us were thinking, which specifically was, "Jesus, we need you. We need your help. Without you, we don't have a chance."

Jesus looks steadfastly as Rocky, nods and says, "I am ready and willing. Believe me, this is the day of victory!"

Rocky calls the play.

As we brake from the huddle Jesus cries out, "Who are we?!"

All together we loudly scream, "The Lionhearts!"

We line up on the ball. The ball is snapped. Rocky takes three steps back. He fires a dart toward Jesus. Jesus, sprinting across the middle, leaps, reaches out, snags the ball with his fingertips, brings it in to his body!

He's nailed! On the five yard line he's hit again, again, again, another shot, another belt, another blow, again, again, again!

He pushes forward! The Demons are dragging him down! He's being crushed by the incredible, seemingly insurmountable weight of it all!

Just then I hear him yell, "Johnny!"

Jesus is now on the one yard line. He's barely standing. Suddenly, he tosses the ball into the air. It seems to float for minutes. Then it finally lands. Right in my hands! I actually caught the ball! I was amazed!

Instantly the stadium went black. Absolute total darkness for about three seconds.

Darkness you could feel!

I trotted forward. As I stepped across the goal line, all the stadium lights lit back up at once. Sudden, phenomenal, extreme brilliance prevailed! More light than the noonday sun! The whole crowd roared! The fans stomped their feet! It felt like a giant earthquake! The whole Lionheart team ran frantically to the endzone. There was great jubilation! They all embraced me! We all jumped in wild ecstatic joy!

Game over! Lionhearts win 30-28!

As we rejoiced, we soon noticed the Blue Demons were, one by one, removing themselves from the pileup that was on top of Jesus. When the last player stood up, he gave Jesus a vicious kick into the side of his body. Jesus didn't budge. He just lay there, flat in his back, his arms spread wide.

We all circled around him as the Demons strutted off the field. Jesus' eyes were closed. Blood was flowing out of his mouth. Coach Love called us to the bench.

The paramedics came. They rolled Jesus onto a white stretcher. They draped a white sheet over him. They carried him away.

I remembered that Rocky had once told Jesus that he was our real captain and team leader. We now all realized that he was also the glue that held our team together. That he was always absolutely faithful, and true, and devoted, and loyal, to every one of us. It was him that gave us strength, and hope, and assurance. He was our inspiration, our confidence, our very life. He was just altogether "wonderful". What could we possibly accomplish without him?

Our great victory turned out to be bittersweet. Though winning that State Championship with an undefeated record was so very marvelous, I think that each one of us felt like a piece of his soul was missing. We all went home with heavy hearts for Jesus.

Three days after the big game there was a fantastic celebration. It seemed like everybody in town was there. First there was a grand parade. Then we had a really big cookout at the town square. Everyone brought lots and lots of good food and drinks.

The Mayor of Kingston came and presented to our team an incredibly huge trophy. It was so big that it took three strong men to carry it.

Then, suddenly, out of nowhere, this kid walks up with a bright glowing smile on his face. He says, "That's a real nice trophy, but all of you, my brothers, are the true trophies."

"It's Jesus!" we shouted!

An overwhelming feeling of joy filled my heart!

The whole team fanatically lifted Jesus up as he raised the victory trophy high to the sky in triumph!

United, we all proclaimed, "Long live the Lionhearts!"

As we celebrated together, all of the townspeople raised their arms straight up into the air, and with sincere reverence and honor, loudly shouted in agreement.

Exactly like the officials do when they signal for a game winning, "Touchdown!" TOUCHDOWN!

MY FAVORITE TEAMMATE IS THE KID NAMED JESUS

Two thousand years ago there lived a true kid named Jesus. You can read about him in the Bible, the holy living Word of God. His father in heaven sent him to the earth to live and to die. Then, he raised him up again, in order that he may deliver all people from all evil. Please take the time to learn about him, for that Jesus alone, is the Lord, and the Savior of the World!

www.ingramcontent.com/pod-product-compliance
Lightning Source LLC
Chambersburg PA
CBHW060346080526
44583CB00014B/1078